Intro from the author and writer...

One of the key requirements to writing su
right words to put in the poems that you are writing when you are writing
them. If you don't choose the right words, and put them in the right
places in the sentences that you're writing, then you can't hope to write
a poem that is succinct, pin-sharp, good and, you know, straight to the
heart of the poem and the people that you're trying to write your poem
for. It's like washing a dog or making a quiche: if you don't put the right
ingredients in the oven, or in the sink where you're trying to shampoo
your pet, then all hellfire will break loose and there'll be a moment where
you think, blimey – that's no good. And the dog's probably got fed up
and disappeared, and you've got nothing for your tea.

So, this is a book that has some poems in it that have been put into it to
make a book of poetry full of poems. It's a book that I've been planning
to construct whilst pretending to teach English in the north of England
for ages, weeks really. It's a book with poems in it that are northern in
their oeuvre and lighthearted in their wordly wordishness. Yes, there are
some really oblique and hard to understand ones in here, like 'By the
Bins', which is about... well, you'll have to try hard with that one. And
there are others about Christmas decorations and Bingo which might
test you (to be honest, they should really be in the Tate Modern some of
these). But don't worry, there are some easy ones too that even the
thickest member of your family should understand. There's one about
shoes that even I can figure out, and another about dancing and buying
stuff and Wigan and buckets. So, there's something for everyone here
really, but you're going to have to read it maybe four or seven times
(possibly even more than that) in order to get anything from it.

So, will it fit in your hand? Yep. Will it make you laugh? Dunno. Will it
change your life? Probably. Will you be able to get a spider on it under a
glass and then chuck it out your back door? Yeah, I reckon. Will it fit
under a wobbly table leg? Or chair leg? Depends.

Look, another thing about this book are the cartoons. Now they were
done by Mr Mark Bardsley. He's a really nice chap who does brilliant
cartoons and you can catch up with him here:
www.markbardsleyillustration.co.uk

And you can find me on Facebook or stay in touch with me here and let
me know if you liked the stories...poem things, whatever:
steve@jiggerypoetry.com
www.jiggerypoetry.com

Northern Nuggets

A Midsummer's Ice Cream

The course of true love never did run smooth
For Gary and Kaz on the van.
She was the sprinkles on his 99
And he was her ice cream man.

Through the streets of the north, they had ruled uncontested
And everyone knew theirs was best.
But things were to change in that long hot July
When their love faced the ultimate test.

Italian vans were always a threat
With their opera and exotic ices.
And trendy sharp shades and smiles from the Med
And over-competitive prices.

But people round here, they knew what they liked -
Not flash with the money they made.
And this latest Romantic to challenge poor Gaz
Had his eye on more than his trade.

Luigi it was, with his tan and gelato
And eyes that lit up the street.
And try as she might, Kaz fell under his spell
And quickly they made plans to meet.

But no screwball was Gaz, he knew what was what
So he followed them into the forest.
Of her love, he was sure, so he took a detour
And bought her some daffs from the florist.

Then there in a clearing, against the low sun,
In the scent of Italian cologne,
Kaz, in the twilight, stared at her new man
And Luigi held out a cone.

"Don't take that ice cream! He's a trickster," yelled Gaz,
As he sped through the brambles and trees.
And armed with some lollies, he jumped from the van
As cool as a blue Mr Freeze.

Kaz ran for cover; she knew what came next
As our hero reached for his pocket.
And poised like a fighter, he drew back his arm
And launched his first raspberry rocket.

Luigi just laughed when the second one came,
Amused by the Englishman's folly.
But Gaz with his pride and some back up munitions,
Took aim with a strawberry lolly.

He caught the Italian right on his nose
And knocked him straight onto the floor.
Blood drizzled down his Armani apron
And he staggered back through his van door.

The forest grew still as the sun disappeared.
Had the visitor now met his match?
But the scene burst to life and when Gaz turned to look,
Luigi jumped down through his hatch.

Cornets of every size flew through the air -
A rainbow of Napoli's best
Limone, pistachio, tiramisu -
Granola, caffe and the rest.

A cider from Gaz with a choc ice to follow,
A blackcurrant Fab and a flake
But Luigi replied with a stracciatella,
And frozen Italian cake.

Deep into the night, the warriors fought,
Until both nothing more they could stand.
But Gaz rose to his feet and faced up to his foe
With an icy grenade in his hand.

The Jubbly of Orange. The four-pointed bomb.
The deadliest ice in the van.
Corners of steel and razor-sharp edges -
Not one you'd take home to your gran.

And in the dawn's light as the dew kissed the ground,
Gaz hurled his last chance at the clown.
Then there in the distance, beyond the tall trees,
He saw the Italian fall down.

Kaz looked at Gaz and Gaz met her eyes
Then they watched 'til Luigi was gone
Then like fallen ice creams on a street in the sun
They melted together as one.

To the Jaffa Cake

O Jaffa Cake, my Jaffa Cake!
No other treat from the shelf I take
Not Kit Kat, Club or Oreo
Nor Jammiest of Dodger go
Into my shopping basket bare
It's the Jaffa Cake that's first in there
There is no other of its ilk

And I only came in for milk.

She Don't Eat Pies

She don't eat pies and that's no lie;
I nearly dropped my Vimto when I found the reason why.
So I gawped at my girl with a look of disgust -
When she said she don't eat things with a crust.

I knew that our relationship was up a cul-de-sac,
So I caught the bus to Argos and took the ring back.
I couldn't settle down with a pie and pasty hater;
She's not the one for me if she spurns meat and potato.

So now I'm on my own and I'm happy with my days;
And I've an envious collection of aluminium trays.
She lives her life on carrots, so I'm glad she disappeared -
I guess some people are a little weird.

What's in a Name?

Don't get a cob on with the Bagel -
The bread-bun with a hole.
This barmcake, bread-bap, tea-cake,
Batch or bun without a soul.

The stottie minus centre;
A lardy-cake, but lame.
It may be incomplete,
But at least it knows its name

The Pool

Cathedral of the speedoed; a mecca for the youth.
See you at the swimming baths - the chamber of the truth.
We're standing proud on Main Street; get here by bus or car
To the darkest side of town to discover who you are.

Lose your inhibitions at our uni-changing doors.
Dislocate your shoulder as you slide upon our floors.
Read the markered love affairs on lockers with no locks:
A place to lose your innocence; a place to lose your socks.

A length or two in our pool will never be forgotten;
No one knows our depth though as you'll never see the bottom.
And you won't find hummus wraps in the caff with Ann or Maureen.
Just ham or cheese or tuna with that added hint of chlorine.

So come and grab a half-chewed float you northern sons and
daughters
And splutter up and down our slightly yellow, freezing waters.
And for the narcissistic or the borough's more transcendent:
Four death-defying diving boards; one YTS attendant.

So sneak under the turnstiles on a Friday after school,
And bomb into the deep end at your local council pool.
And when you've earned your Monster Munch and dodged the towel-
flickers,
Walk out a different person, wearing someone else's knickers.

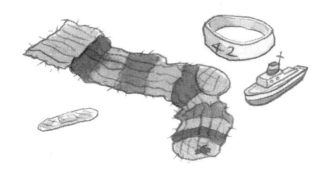

Blame it on the Buggy

It couldn't be no bad thing, the go-cart challenge that spring,
When half the world came out to see us ride.
And feeling what a man feels - on rusted, buckled pram wheels,
We hurtled down the crescent side by side.

And showing me the way to go, the older kids like Craig and Joe
Were tearing streets of this estate apart.
But Big Daz, working day and night to get the combination right,
Had made a beast that almost stopped your heart.

Like something from a movie scene, that Daz caressed his beauty
queen
And held that bend with icy cool demeanour.
But me, just like a snooker ball, went ricocheting off the wall
And smashed into a static Ford Cortina.

With nose all squashed, too small for face, and mouth contorted out of
place,
I knew right then my buggy race was run.
And lying there with crying eyes, and feeling not like other guys,
I wondered if I'd ever see the sun.

Some blamed it on the sunshine; some blamed it on the noon light -
But all my schemes and plans had gone awry.
And in the dumps and feeling strange, I knew I'd have to make a
change,
So on that night I kissed that cart goodbye.

Born to Rub

In the day we sweat it out with the scratch cards in our hand.
A three, two fives, a six for Friday night.
And perched outside the Co-op with a coke and Chunky KitKat,
We dream that one day we can make it right.

Within an hour, we're back for more with money we don't have;
We caress another three outside the pub.
And leaning on the wall, we know we'll never break this trap,
'Cos maybe tramps like us were born to rub.

Northern Sole

How did you get there oh size 13 Clarks
On the road between Scarborough and York?
From where did you come?
Were you dropped from up high?
Were you thrown from a bridge?
Did you walk?

O tell of your journey oh hard shoulder shoes
As I slow to a queue in the lane.
Were you flung from the window?
Or sun-roof ejected?
Was it anger that made
Feet become disconnected?
And now on your side
You're exposed, unprotected.
Outcasts, alone in the rain.

How long will you kick around lost in the gutter
Oh mystical shoes in a pair?
Off duty coach drivers,
Time on their hands;
Three abreast workmen
In Volkswagen vans;
Children on backseats
Three hours from gran's
Amazed and dumbfounded
At roadside footwear
(Abandoned, rejected,
in need of repair)
Will mumble the question
That hangs in the air:
How the hell did those size 13 Clarks
End up there?

Tribute Tribute

Let's hear it for the tribute band: raise glasses if you would.
A bit like all your favourite groups but nowhere near as good.
Find them in the church hall on a Tuesday in November
And tell yourself the singer beats the one that you remember.

A geordie Robbie Williams, David Bowie with a lisp,
Sway to George Recycle as you tuck into your crisps.
The Rolling Clones will start you up; Dead Zepplin take you higher;
The Back Doors or an overweight Fake That will light your fire.

A balding Freddie Mercury, a Michael Jackson rip-off,
A three-star Elton John we're all beginning to get sick of.
The Beatles and The Hollies with their phony doppelgängers;
An awful Liam Gallagher that's turned up to harangue us.

So long live all the tributes with their spandex and their covers.
Give us that kind of magic now we cannot get the others.
We'll book you for the garden fete and love you in the pub.
And we'll make believe it's Wembley when it's Bury Labour Club.

Ode to The Pie Shop

Step out from the confines of counter;
Hot foot it from construction site.
Reject midday view from the scaffold
And march to the source of the light.

Get away from the grey of the office;
Abscond from the hullabaloo.
Meet pilgrimage friends aplenty
In the pie shop's lunchtime queue.

A conga of north camaraderie,
A scrumpled up list and a pen:
For the boss, sausage rolls and two doughnuts;
Steak and kidney and Fanta times ten.

Donna and Linda are ready,
Standing firm between flapjack and bun.
A large piece of pizza, a pasty,
A pie in a barm on the run.

So gather, you northern-bound townies;
Put down those tools, make a brew.
And savour the anticipation
In the pie-shop lunchtime queue.

Kayli

Marillions of crystals for our treat on Friday night.
A rainbow in a bag for us to share.
Kayli, my Kayli, oh I never thought I'd miss you -
And bitter is my stick of spanish now that you're not there.
Dolly mixtures, cherry lips and cola cubes ignored;
Those chocolate limes, they knew you were the one.
And Kayli I thought that we would always be good friends
But it seems you're more important now you're gone.

Stretchy Jeans

The last pair that I had were stiff like corrugated iron.
Could hardly reach my trainers when my laces needed tying.
I'd done a bit of overtime so found I had the means,
To jump the bus last Sunday for a brand new pair of jeans.

It's ages since I'd bought some, so there's things that I'd forgotten -
(Had spent the last three decades in some Kappa tracksuit bottoms.)
So when the moment came to trundle in behind the curtain,
I took in sixteen pairs and fourteen belts just to be certain.

An hour later, sweating cobs and feeling rather ill,
I staggered through this darkened shop to Charmayne on the till.
And with my cool and trendy brand new denims in my hand,
Puffed out my chest and strutted down the street a different man.

That night down at the bingo though, another joy I found.
As when Lynne dropped her dibber, I was first down on the ground.
The grimacing and groans I used to feel with such an action
Were now supplanted by a more elasticated traction.

The dance floor, in my old ones, well I wouldn't have a prayer,
But wearing these new jeans, I kicked both legs up in the air.
No more that stabbing feeling when the fabric cut my thighs,
Even Alan selling bingo tickets couldn't believe his eyes.

All evening I was moving like a keep-fit superstar;
It was lunges in the toilets and squat-thrusts at the bar
(Gary told me jeans these days contained a touch of Lycra,
And that was why I found it easy getting out the Micra.)

But laid in bed that night I tossed and turned and couldn't rest;
Until it dawned upon me, as I stripped down to my vest.
I bolted upright, turned the light on, felt my whole world spinning
And realised perhaps I'd bought those ones for pregnant women.

Silent Disco

Gary, for his fortieth, he kept us in the dark,
As we had no idea about this silent disco lark.
We packed away the dominoes and jumped down off the bus,
As Gary put us straight and told us not to cause a fuss.

Independent listening, not a DJ with a mike;
You just pop some headphones on and bop around to what you like.
He told us times were changing, as we looked at him and smiled;
And Alan dropped his crisps when he found they didn't serve mild.

A futuristic vision stopped us firmly in our tracks,
As my fingers slowly tightened in the pockets of my slacks:
Everyone was wired up and shuffling around,
Like a Friday evening freak show or the telly with no sound.

A group of girls with eyes shut clearly didn't care a jot
As they pirouetted wildly round the floor to god knows what.
And a bloke without his shirt on danced to something from the charts
When Danny from the bar announced they hadn't any darts.

But soon we all got up and did that 'to the dance floor' dance:
Andy with his Motown on and Dennis with his trance.
Brian did the Macarena, Martin did the twist
And Colin bounced to Dexy's Midnight Runners' Greatest Hits.

Geoff was waking up to Wham and breaking free to Queen;
Rob and Dave where swaying round to Marvin and Al Green.
Mickey in his one white glove was positively gone
And moonwalking around the place like he was twenty one.

However, things got sticky near the toilets, around ten;
As someone in the one-man conga clattered into Ben.
This silent dancing's one thing, but I could have wound up dead
When I tumbled over Ian, doing Oops Upside Your Head.

Gary said the night had turned out better than he'd planned,
While Carl and Craig and Big Daz Agadoo-ed and Wigwam-Bammed.
But Paul, who'd brought his iPod just ignored this room of mime -
And tuned into his podcasts of Gardeners' Question Time.

Profiterole Vision

At the edges, on the fringes
Is where my self-restraint unhinges,
For in the corner of my eye,
Lurks that cream and cherry pie.

Lose the function of my legs,
At any shop that looks like Greggs,
As in the window's winter sun:
Fruity flapjack, Chelsea bun,

A custard tart, a chocolate brownie -
Fudged confessions of a townie.
Vanilla slice, jam sponge, eclair,
Just in the window, waiting there.

On the blindside still they linger,
Point their pinkened icy finger.
Resist temptation? Hit the brake?
Wish it was a piece of cake.

Another One Bites the Crust

They do things different in Wigan
Of that they can't deny
Rugby, chips and Bingo
Are things that get them high.
But the icing on the cake is -
And I'm not one to lie -
A round or square, not to share,
Shop-bought crusty pie.

They'd kill you for a pie,
Yes they'd kill you for a pie.
For pudding, chips and gravy
They would poke you in the eye.
For a can of fizzy Vimto,
It's a compass in your thigh.
But cross my heart and hope to die,
They'd kill you for a pie.

I walked through Wigan's centre

Forlorn and uninspired.
I'd caught the bus from Bolton -
I was feeling very tired.
So I bought a chicken pie
And found a bench to rest my legs,
But I could see them eye my greaseproof bag
As I came out of Greggs.

Oh they'd kill you for a pie,
Yes they'd kill you for a pie.
For a quarter bag of cola cubes,
They'd whip you with their tie.
For a clutch of penny chews
They'd find a way to make you cry.
For a 1am kebab
They'd surely hang you out to dry.
And I just simply don't know why
In Wigan senses go awry
When desperate for a new supply -
They'd kill you for a pie.

Bit Pricey Flower

I'm on my way to Chelsea:
The flowers, not the footy.
For Monty Don and Carol Klein,
It's true I turn to putty.
My friends from here up north
Are convinced I'm rather nutty
'Cos it's £4 for a cup of tea
And eight quid for a butty!

Bienvenue
(In praise of the cafe at B&Q)

Stop for a flapjack, a teacake, a brew.
The aroma of coffee and toast is the cue.
Step out of the chaos and hullabaloo.
Our bright orange aprons are waiting for you.

What will it be sir? A table for two?
Chillax in the corner; take in the view.
See there in the distance the filler, the glue -
The foreground adorned by the nail and the screw.

Comprehensive selection of carpet shampoo.
Beyond there, the compost - John Innes number two.
There's the pipe that you carelessly put a nail through
And the bathroom displays: 10% off a loo.

And the rivers of paint: the turquoise, the blue,
Complimentary colour chart one can leaf through.
Kaleidoscope hues: a bespoke Xanadu.
As you sip at your latte, would you write a review?

Whilst assessing the Do It Yourself you can do
Our romantic cafe will make you feel new.
Find us on Facebook, in Bolton or Crewe -
We're next to the gents, at your B&Q.

B&Q Blues

She said,
"Pick a blue, something light
That goes with the blind but not too bright.
Something morning, something cool,
Something hotel swimming pool.
Something simple, something plain,
Like your shirt but not the same.
That colour we looked at once, you know,
In Homes and Gardens years ago.
A touch of aquamarine, no more -
A bit more chic than her's next door.
Bluish blue - look, it's time I was gone.
Anything really, you choose one."

So here I am, in B&Q
Staring at a million types of blue:
Snorkeling Trip, December Solstice,
Blue Bolero- who knows what this is?
Windswept Clouds, Parrot Flight,
Cool Box, Journey into Night,
Coastal Waters, Easy Breeze -
How much are they paid to come up with these?
Frosty Snowcap, Dover Shore,
Summer Rain, Ocean Floor,
Arctic Sunrise, Fairy Cup,
God's Toothpaste - no, I made that up.
Midnight Magic, Moroccan Sky,
Seize the Day, Flying High.
I'm on a roller now, try stop me.
More shades of blue than types of coffee.
Enough to put you in a trance.
Paint the bathroom? No chance.

So empty-handed I drove home.
Praying that she wouldn't phone
To check on progress, colour, sheen.
A quick update, know what I mean?
I staggered in and made a brew
And surveyed the scene from on the loo.
For me, our bathroom looked alright
Why the change? What's wrong with white?

All afternoon the floor I'm pacing,
Cold sweats while I'm watching racing.
How would it go? What would she say
About my unproductive day?

And then at six: the drive, her car.
My hand flew to my jugular
As she flew up to check the room
And descended stoney-faced too soon.
Her piercing eyes said it all
(I feared I'd end up on the wall.)

"Darling, there were just too many.
I froze, I panicked and didn't choose any."

She brushed me off with just one stare
And left me standing lonely there.
My colour drained; I started itching
As she summoned me into the kitchen.
By then, my legs were quite unstable
And spread before me on the table
Rows and rows of colour charts.
"This is where your nightmare starts,"
She said without a hint of fun.
"By 3am , we'll have the one."

So ahead a night of paint fatigue.
No feet up, crisps and Champions League.
I fained interest but she could tell
I wasn't feeling very well.
But then beneath the kitchen light
Bizarrely, no blue card in sight.
She chirped, when asked what did it mean:
"I've changed my mind. We're having green.

Stuck in the Middle

Hondas by the hundred and a million Yamahas.
He parks himself and ticks off coaches, motorbikes and cars.
A trillion transits trundle down to Manchester from Leeds;
A zillion caravans are spied at catch the ferry speeds.

I'm married to the farm that splits the damn M62.
But what gets him excited are the trucks that thunder through.
My heart is full of longing as a limousine seems full
Of young 'uns on a hen-do, off to Liverpool from Hull.

Notebooks break the shelves and spreadsheets cover every table.
And each day brings another multicoloured graph to label.
But notice me, he never does, however hard I try.
He just legs it down the meadow when a wide-load passes by.

I tell him that we mustn't let this roadside living test us,
That he shouldn't lose his heart to spotting Corsas and Fiestas.
But I gaze at him and know that we're about to fall apart -
As he shades another column on his Eddie Stobbart chart.

Life in the Fast Lane

The man in the farm on the M62
In pyjamas in morning dew, sipping his brew,
What goes through his mind as he takes in the view
Of the sunrise over the M62?

The plans that they drew and the money they threw:
Does the farmer regret not thinking it through?
And after the chaos and hullabaloo,
Does he think that he's bitten more than he chew?

Or, as you're crawling to Leeds in the queue,
To the heat of the office you'll never get to,
Does he smirk at the traffic that trundles askew
Round his triumphant farm on the M62?

So, is it for me? Or is it for you?
If the hard hats came calling out of the blue
And threw down the same issue, what would you do
With your farm in the middle of the M62?

Eyes Down

Barbara keeps her head down at the bingo here tonight.
Three wins on the spin suggests that something isn't right.
A line, a house last weekend and the jackpot week before
Has left her friends from Slimming Club questioning the score.

So when the tension mounts on the evening's opening card,
And the women from the salon grip their dibbers extra hard.
As the caller takes his place, he knows precisely what's at stake:
Another win for Barbara would be difficult to take.

The house lights dim as Alan draws the mike up to his lips;
Our hero sits with Val and helps her finish off her chips.
And as the numbers tumble, Barbara senses waiting knives
From the pie shop girls across the room, dibbing for their lives.

But Barbara isn't one to let some scallies from the town
Bully her and make her put that purple marker down.
She's worshipped at these tables for all her working years;
No painted lady cafe girls can bring this one to tears.

But seriously, what will she do if Alan calls her number?
Shout 'house' and claim the win and find a table to climb under?
Or will she take the easy way when finding she was near it?
Delve in her bag? Nip to the loo? Pretend she didn't hear it?

Poor Barbara starts to shiver as her card gets down to one:
Her pen poised on the button to release the atom bomb.
Kelly's Eye to win the game and set off World War III,
Or keep her mouth shut, let it pass and and hold some dignity.

In silence everybody knows that something bad is hatching,
As the smell of danger hovers over lager and pork scratchings.
But when Barbara looks at Alan and gives a little cough,
Alan gets the signal and things totally kick off.

"I knew it," bellows Angie, "I knew you'd bloody cheated!
I won't come here again," she yells, "I've never been worse treated."
Then others join the chaos and some wine glasses are thrown,
And Donna says she'll strangle Alan with that microphone.

Cheryl flips a table and Sharon throws a chair
And Pauline from the betting shop grabs hold of Vicky's hair.
Maureen puts the boot in on Karen from the Spar,
While Andrea the owner pulls the shutters on the bar.

In the violence and the brawling, Al and Barbara seize their moment;
Disinterested in coming clean, confessions or atonement.
As women, booze and blood and hair pour through the fire exit,
Babs hoists Alan in the air, grabs the cash and legs it.

Slip Up (To the Winter Olympics)

Can't fail to be impressed by luge or skeleton or bob.
Or wowed by downhill moguls or the cool ice-hockey mob.
And who don't feel the tension when those curlies do their pushes?
In their slippy-slidey trainers with their whizzy little brushes.

The death-defying slalom racers, jumpers and snowboarders;
The pricey-sunglassed, bobble-hatted, drippy-nosed applauders.
And round their mugs of special tea, Claire Balding, Hazel Irvine
Take us through the sliding, slipping, slicing, skidding, swerving.
But let's not be complacent with the wondrous pirouette -
Things that seem quite perfect could be made a bit more better.
For even though we love the views and icy cool transmission,
A bit more North of England would improve this competition:

What's up with lobbing snowballs at your sister or your brother?
Or skimming school bags down the street from one end to the other?
Or sledging down the field on bits of wood or plastic bags.
Or splitting open heads on deadly, icy garden flags?

A tournament where dads scrape ice from off a Ford Granada;
Perhaps put them in slippers just to make it a bit harder.
A moan about the gritter game where two teams disagree;
A build-a-snowman race before a mum shouts them for tea.

A billion worldwide winter sporting fans can't fail to love
A chase around the house in search of woolly hat and glove.
And for the more discerning fan who likes the off-piste feature,
A contest throwing ice balls at a playground-cornered teacher.

So let me on the IOC, and watch me take control;
Let's warm this icy combo with a touch of northern soul.
And if those sporty chieftains don't respond well to our needs,
We'll hold our own in Bradford, Wakefield, Huddersfield or Leeds.

No Woman, No Pie

A moment on the lips, Dawn;
Don't forget your goals.
You know that you'll regret it
If you have those sausage rolls.

Forget the cakes and flapjacks,
They're no good for your health.
And take your greedy eyes
Off them pasties on the shelf.

Put the Fanta down, Dawn,
Unless you need the pounds;
The bakewell and the brownie
And the doughnut's out of bounds.

A week away from Greggs, Dawn
Won't mean you'll fade away.
You've got the wrong idea, Dawn,
About this five a day.

Co-op FM

Secret room above a shop in Wigan.
Up at 5.30 and always on the go.
I come down on my bike,
Get free Hob Nobs when I like -
I'm the DJ on the Co-op radio.

Here's one from Lionel Rich Tea, I'm certain that you'll know,
Followed by a track from Radiobread.
And while you choose your greens,
It's Dexy's Midnight Runner Beans
Or a bit of Hall and Porridge Oats instead.

I play them all I do, as you shuffle round the shelves:
Bananarama while you're choosing ham.
All your favourites of that ilk
Can serenade you near the milk,
On the way past Dolly Parkin and The Jam.

Towered tins of Guns and Roses join you in your quest
Or Michael Buble-gum could take you higher.
But if you like your 70s' beats,
Try Ziggy Starburst near the sweets.
If not, perhaps Cake That can light your fire.

Or if you're in for pâté, maybe classical's your bag:
Procoffee-ev, Quorn Williams - that's the gist.
Best shop we surely shall be
'Cos you don't get this VivAldi -
High culture while you scan your Chopin Liszt.

So come down to the Co-op for your radio with taste;
From Crisps de Burgh to Simon le Bon Bon.
You can make requests at will;
Ask Tina Turnip on the till.
Be quick though as she's out The Doors at one.

Gift Shops

Quite like castles and stately homes,
Old buildings throughout the land.
Museums make me feel dead smart,
But gift shops I can't stand.

Shelves of shortbread, tartan tins,
Books on keeping bees.
Embroidered cushion covers,
Alan Titchmarsh DVDs.
Christmas jigsaws, painted eggs,
Coasters by the crate
Volunteers with homely names,
Mugs of Princess Kate.

So when I'm lost in cookbooks
And CDs from World War One
It takes all my British spirit
To keep calm and carry on.

Home Truths

Just Desserts

Another rejection this morning.
This time the Royal Philharmonic.
Last week the Halle
Then the Royal ballet -
Before that, the New York Symphonic.

Applications to all the big hitters,
But I can't seem to get an audition
To show them I'm able
With soup, tea or table -
Can't see that there's much competition.

But it looks like there's no room for spoons,
As composers ignored their potential.
Vivaldi and Bach
With the strings made their mark,
Yet neglected this tuneful utensil.

Well, I've had it with those virtuosos.
Last chance is the famous Royal College
And if they're not for switchin'
To sounds from the kitchen.
I'll go back to ice cream and porridge.

Trampoline Club

There it stands in the corner of the lawn
Hovering three feet above bare ground.
Kids these days, they don't know they're born;
The springs are all shot and the netting is torn
But I climb in when no-one's around.

An anti-gravity cage of delight;
The cathedral of fun by the wall.
My daughter and wife are out for the night
And I decide, as I bounce with all my might,
To give Mickey and Alan a call.

And Dave and Tony and Chris and Dean
And Jimmy and Martin and Pete.
And before too long we've got a routine
With backdrops and spins like we are thirteen
Slowing the years in bare feet.

Soon though, our evening is over.
Dave's hurt his back and I've bit my tongue
And Alan's front teeth are lodged in Dean's head
Mick's had enough; his face is all red.
And we can't remember which one of us said:
"It's best to leave youth to the young.

Our Neighbours Have Got a Jacuzzi

Our neighbours have got a jacuzzi
On their patio, near the back door.
It whirrs and it bubbles;
It bubbles and hums;
It hums and it rumbles
'Til darkness comes.
It slices the night like a knife through butter -
I can barely hear my hedge-cutter.

The sound of it drives me insane;
They chill in bikini and shorts.
And they chat and they dip;
They dip and they drink;
They drink and they chink
I can't hear myself think
And my face is becoming more redder
As I'm loading stuff into my shredder.

It purrs and it whizzes;
It whizzes and foams;
It foams and it froths
And it froths and it drones
And it drones and it drones
While they play on their phones.
I have tried throwing stones
In the evening, just before dinner
So I plug in the Bosch garden strimmer

It's getting me down
That detestable sound
Of friendly chit-chat
When they've got their friends round.
That drip drip effect
Is pure torture to me.
I can't hear my mower
Or my JCB.
I'm planning to move house soon.
I could do with a quiet afternoon.

Easter Egg Hunt

My dad thought he was funny;
The Easter Egg Hunt was a flop.
After days of searching the house,
He revealed they were still in the Co-op.

Hip Op

Only went round for Geoff's ladders.
And there by the open shed door:
Propped up by the bikes and the strimmer,
A piece of lino from his old kitchen floor.

The kids were at footy and Linda was out
So he bounded upstairs for his tapes:
Grand Master Flash, Run DMC -
As I began shaping some shapes.

We flattened it out on the patio,
And checked there was no-one around.
With baseball caps twisted, we stood face to face
And pointed straight down at the ground.

Soon we were popping and scratching and locking
Garden chairs rocking - our joints began knocking
And Geoff's on his knees, lost in the ecstasy
Sliding and gliding and moonwalking next to me
Jerking and jumping and jacking his body
(Can't move like this to Showaddywaddy).
Here comes his jackhammer, windmill, back spin.
Rolling back years between tulips and wheelie bin.
Boomerangs, elbow hops, freeze and a flare.
Head spins were easier when we had hair.

But the swallow-dive into the caterpillar
Did for Geoff and his hip and his knee.
The ambulance came about two-ish
To blue-light him to A&E.

A four hour wait, then the nurse came
And we both knew what she would say:
After finding Geoff's name on her clipboard,
She told him to walk this way.

Before the News

Glued all afternoon to Lesley Judd and Peter Purvis,
Roy Castle, Johnny Ball and Rentaghost.
Dinner skipped for footy with the big kids on the yard,
And now fish fingers, chips or beans on toast.

But while mum in the kitchen drowns in clatter and in steam,
And the thump of plate on table we refuse,
We sink into the sofa to steal the last five minutes
For that little programme just before the news.

Cue Ivor the Engine, Captain Pugwash, Willo the Wisp;
Orinocco, Tomsk and Tobermory
Paddington and Rhubarb, Custard, Florence, Doogle, Dylan -
The bookend to our every weekday story.

And mum knows what we're up as we squeeze the last few seconds
Of the multicoloured stop-motion performer.
And she lets us Womble free; and for now resist our tea,
For she knows real life lurks just around the corner.

Sticky Moments

In the days before wet-wipes,
Those medieval times,
Mum had clever ways
To make our mouths and faces shine.

A simple gun-sling action
With a mother's quickfire spin
To cure the juice around our lips
Or ice cream on our chin,

The chocolate on our fingers
Or the biscuit in our eyes;
Or the remnant crumbs upon our cheeks
From flakey pastry pies.

Our lunchtime misdemeanours
Never made our mam too cranky
As she delved into her pocket,
Grabbed our heads and licked a hanky.

Names

We lived our lives as Poppet, Pudding, Chucky Egg, Sweet Pea.
Tilly Mint or Flossy when they shouted us for tea.
And when we said too much or got too big or pushed our luck,
They'd put us in our place with Buggerlugs or Lady Muck.

Then Jack the Lad or Donut wouldn't fail to wind us up.
And coming off the field, It's Dirty Harry, Mucky Pup.
They'd called us Queen or Princess, Bobby Dazzler for a laugh!
And Joe Soap on a Sunday when we'd got out of the bath.

Pumpkin, Petal, Flowerpot, Our Kid and Dolly Daydream,
Tuppence, Pet or Shilling as they'd sit us on their knee.
We answer to these names still, but know that none compares
To when our mam and dad embrace us now and call us theirs.

Bin Day

In the distance that familiar sound;
He under sheets in the heat.
Then a jolt and realisation
That the bin lorry was in the next street.

Explodes from bed and flies downstairs -
A trembling blur of fear.
The seconds ticked like bombs;
The iron man pulled near.

A curse and scramble for the keys,
He knew this one was tight.
The cat had run for cover
As dad burst into the light.

What caused him to forget that day
His duties, as a man?
Why so did he refuse to scan
His refuse collection plan?
Was it time that took its toll
And turned his aged brain to jelly?
Or raw fatigue or overwork
Or last night's football on the telly?
Hydraulic jaws were closer then,
The morning filled with racket
Of clanking, thundering metal arms
And men in yellow jackets.

He dragged the bins with sweating hands
At top speed down the drive.
(And in these magic moments
Ain't it great to be alive?)

And when they rested by the gate,
He stood with burning pride.
Eyeballs filled with joyous tears
And nerves electrified.

So he ran and spun and thumped his chest
In the early morning breeze.
And like a scoring number nine,
Slid down the street on his knees.

His shouts and whoops increased
Before that truck had even gone.
And he'd have taken all his clothes off
If he'd have had any on.

Sunday Tea

Unreasonably excited when we see the cheese on sticks;
Lifeless weekend reignited: Sunday, half past six.
Nest of tables, previously stranded by the door,
Shuffled by my sister to the middle of the floor.

Mum rolls out the Jacob's crackers, sandwiches and ham,
The Philly and the corned beef, pickled onions and the spam.
Carnation milk, tinned peaches and a rabbit-moulded jelly.
The big light's on, the fire's up and Bullseye's on the telly.

No doubt other families have their rituals like we do.
A custom that belongs to them that no one else can see through.
But Sunday tea at our house really was the stuff of dreams -
And we thought we'd gone to heaven when mum brought out the
custard creams.

Dad's Ponytail

I thought I'd done a real good job:
Gathered the hair from left and right,
A bobble on my wrist,
No tears or shouting out.
She puts up with me when mum's not about.
Brushed it back with a twist
And rapidly flicked the bobble over
And over and over
Carefully in line with where the hair was parted.

But that's where the trouble started.
Instead of being happy with an adequate result,
I pulled at the hair, like a catapult
And forced another circle of elastic
To cram that ponytail in.
But fantastic it was not.
What began dead central,
Now was skewed,
And in need of something drastic.
What I should have done was start again
To eliminate the ensuing pain -
Is what my only daughter said.
But foolishly
Yet coolishly
I pushed the whole thing round a bit
And tried to change the shape of her head.

I Would Do Anything for Love - But I Can't Do Plaits

(or Plait Out of Hell)

Mum's up and gone at the first crack of dawn.
Sorted washing and then fed the cat.
But my daughter of four
Arrives dressed at the door
And says, "Dad, I could do with a plait."

"A what?" I replied as my blood ran cold,
And my fingers started to clench.
"A plait. You know, hair?
The brush is just there.
And dad, get a grip, make it French."

I Fought the Lawn

Pegging out the washing in November's sinking sun,
A slight but steady breeze up in the trees.
A day or two of dryness has me looking at the lawn -
One last cut before the winter freeze?

Neglected since September and that final barbecue;
Ignored for Halloween and Bonfire Night.
But now, as Bosch's finest purrs from garage darkness deep,
Today's the day I put this garden right.

Tufts like mines, lie waiting near the border at the back,
Unnoticed in the shadow by the hedge
Glistening grass pricks moisture through my trainers to my skin,
As balanced tea grows cold on window ledge.

A yard or two, or five at most, before the mower's over
And screwdriver or stick begin to poke.
Then up again, and in reverse I trudge towards the fence
And ignore the smell of burning and of smoke.

And mocking tea sits smugly in the evening's biting chill,
And figures in the kitchen start to hover.
And winding in the lead I know that soon I'll have to face
Those eyes that seem to scream: "Why did you bother?"

And was it worth the energy, the cursing and the sweat,
The battle with the brave but bound-up blade?
In Autumn's creeping twilight, I squint into the gloom
And gaze upon the bloody mess I've made.

Caravan of Love

Three days of torrential rain
Tried it's best to spoil it.
A quagmire round the steps
And a blocked up chemical toilet.
A pitch four miles from showers -
Almost all of that uphill.
Llandudno sites were taken
So we ended up in Rhyl.

But the romance of the open road,
The life-affirming sky,
The highlife in the slow lane
With the summer whizzing by,
The fourteen hour stretches
That never seemed that long
Only proved that mum and dad were right
And all of us were wrong.

Runaway

A runaway trolley in the car park in ASDA
Makes a dash from the boot of a hungry grey Mazda.
A doubled-up, debutant dad tries to master
The isofix seat as his shopping moves faster.

His Flash and his runner beans aren't up for slowing;
His five-minute rapid cook pasta is going.
The baby and seat he decides to just throw in -
I'd love to help out, but I'm writing this poem.

Mother's Day

Marks and Spencer's flowers, delivered to the door;
Some pricey eau de toilet stuff from Debenham's first floor.
A scarf of silk, a pair of gloves, a jumper off eBay;
Now That's What I Call Mums CD from Amazon UK.

It's easy for me now to list the things I should have bought her;
It would have been a doddle, if I'd have been a daughter.
But I saw her smile subside in the backseat of the car
When I dropped her off last Tuesday for some me-time at the Spar.

The Outing

Our mum, she overdid it
Getting ready for an outing.
Military precision
That rarely turned to shouting.

It was obvious she loved us;
It was clear how much she cared.
And no-one could accuse her
Of going unprepared.

A bag of wholemeal sandwiches,
Crackers in a box.
A dozen packs of knickers,
Ten spare pairs of socks.

Pricey brand new walking boots,
Tee-shirts by the score,
Packed neatly in three cases
And stacked up by the door.

Factor 30 sun cream,
Pens and cards and games.
Baseball caps and jumpers
All labelled with our names.

And when everything was loaded,
We squeezed into the car.
Luggage checked and ready
For our trip out to the Spar.

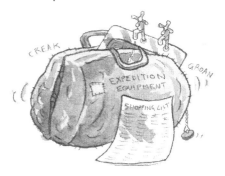

Bring Me Sunshine

Shared out with my sister, half a rabbit-moulded jelly.
Three bars burning on the fire, Russ Abbott on the telly.
A Strongbow for our dad and ready salted for our mam.
Nobody does Saturday night, the way our family can.

Flick the big light off, go on, and pour a glass of coke.
Watch dad light up another and then tell us not to smoke.
Then push the ancient couch into the middle of the room
And savour every second, knowing bedtime's coming soon.

A croon or two from Doonican: there's one that I'd forgot.
We like it when Paul Daniels does his tricks, but not a lot.
We fawn all over Forsyth with his sideburns and his chin,
And we love it when that couple from Cleckheaton win a bin.

So grab another bag of crisps with salt you have to shake;
And marvel at the armoured car that Mr T can make.
Beg and plead to stay up for the horror double bill:
Karloff, Peter Cushing, Vincent Price and Jimmy Hill.

Go mad, kick off your slippers as your eyes begin to fail.
Ask mum to shed some light on Ronnie Corbett's armchair tale.
Hide faces in a cushion if the Daleks get too near.
But save these priceless memories before they disappear.

Anything Really

Buy me some socks. A cliché I know.
But they're really the things
That make my heart sing.
Father's Day, birthdays or under the tree,
Socks from the market will satisfy me.
I know that this pressie don't scream rock n roll,
But there's nothing like socks for the soul.

Get me some hankies. All smart in a box.
When wintertime comes
And my nose starts to run,
To dip in my pocket and pull out a silk one
Satin or cotton, polyester or nylon.
Again, as a present, I can't say it rocks
But I'd love them as much as those socks.

Well get me some vouchers if they're a bit flash.
iTunes for music;
I'm happy to choose it.
My eighties collection could do with a lift -
Now that's what I call a number one gift.
But if that brings you out in a rash,
Forget it, just give me the cash.

Let's Go Fly a Kite

Let's go fly a kite.
The sun is out and the wind's just right.
Come on you two, get out of bed.
It's here I think, near the bikes in the shed.

There's not much to beat the joy it can bring:
Nature's powerful pull on the string.
Majestic and free like a dream on the air;
What must it be to be soaring up there?

Look, keep it simple, no mad acrobatics;
No somersaults, nose-dives, avoid problematics.
Let's learn how to walk before you can run,
And remember, untangling's part of the fun.

Now fly down the field and lift it up slow
Then send it up gently when I say go.
You'd think you were dead with the faces you've got;
I'll give you a turn when I've shown you what's what.

Don't you just love it? This rainbow of power.
This jump jet; this eagle; this giant sunflower.
Its 3 metre tail, you can't fail to admire
As it hangs with the rest on that telegraph wire.

He Didn't Invent It.

You know the one…
The old banana as a phone gag:
Holds it to his ear and winks,
"It's for you."
He didn't invent it,
But that is dad through and through.

You know the one…
The old reflection in a doorway thing:
There he goes, arms and legs
In the air
Half out, half in
Like one of those figures
Where you pull the string.
He didn't create that,
But cut him in half
And dad bleeds that kind of thing.

And flicking a tangerine
Off the elastic crook of his arm
Effortlessly back into his hand.
And conjuring your nose
To appear in his fingers.
And the handkerchief clamped to his face by his glasses.
Handkerchief Man!
And that scary hand that grabs his head from behind the door!

A millionbilliontrillion
GodzillionPrinceWilliam more like that
To excite, entertain,
Startle and stun.

He didn't create these.
But if nobody else had,
He would have done.

Out to Lunch

Gran's face was a picture when they brought her order over
And she felt her hunger pangs disintegrate.
Always one to open up her mind to something new,
But fish and chips and peas served on a slate?

"Old fashioned you can call me," exclaimed Gran, "set in my ways.
I'm fussy and a little bit aloof.
But do they call it style these days to serve up Whitby's finest
On a piece of stone that's fallen off the roof?

She calmed though as the waitress reappeared through double doors,
Weighed down with lunch for seven, table two.
For dad's roast beef and onions stretched out chicly on some carpet
And his French fries nestled snugly in a shoe.

Billy's Jeans

"Have a bit of self-respect.
Pull em up!" said Billy's dad.
"People can see your backside, son -
It just looks really bad."
He rolled his eyes at aunty Val
And said, "There's always one."
Then moonwalked to the fridge
And claimed, "The kid is not my son."

No Hands

When washing car or clipping hedge, his eyes were cast our way;
He spied on us when drying pots and pans.
If they could do it so could he, thought dad that fateful day:
Those scallies riding Choppers with no hands.

So when temptation gripped him and he couldn't stand no more,
He grabbed my bike and pushed it up the hill.
"I'll show them how it's done," he mused with foot paused on the pedal,
As he stood there in the late November chill.

And like Evel Knieval, circa Wembley '75,
Dad was that double-decker-jumping biker;
The neighbours in their windows and our mam stood at the gate
Just thankful that he wasn't dressed in lycra.

A spangled hush; a gentle push and dad was on his way;
At first, an aimless, fragile butterfly.
But as the wheels rolled faster and the breeze caressed his hair,
He raised both nervous hands towards the sky.

I'd love to say that dad became the hero at that moment;
I'd love to reconstruct this episode.
But sadly he resorted to the use of both his hands
When picking up his front teeth from the road.

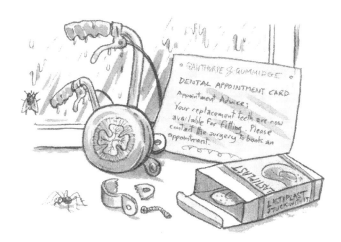

Dads' Race

He pretends he doesn't care
As he steps up to the line.
He stretches and he bends,
And he focuses his mind.

He chases big improvements
From the second place last year.
Trained seven times a week for months
And bought designer gear.

So he tightens up his spikes
And he pulls up both his socks.
And he looks up to the sky
As he settles in his blocks.

Recollections of defeat
Are still too difficult to handle -
Beaten, as he was then
By a grandad in some sandals.
But now a chance for glory
And he's quickly in the zone.
Determination in his eyes,
He switches off his phone.

But all the self-reflection
And this dwelling on the past
Means he doesn't hear the gun go off,
So this year he comes last.

Below Par

How straight it flew. How long it flew.
A heaven sent drive on the third.
Past windmill, o'er bridge,
Full cresting the ridge,
Green eyes gazing on, without word.

Three inches from hole it decided to rest;
Strikes of such style are few.
Casual but sturdy,
With a smile for the birdie,
I caressed it straight home for a two.

On subsequent holes, the same story.
Dream approaches, then in for the kill.
Then a selfie to tweet
'Cos there's nothing to beat
Crazy golf on the seafront at Rhyl.

Jumpstart

Bag crammed with The Sun
On our paper rounds from seven;
Then pulling wheelies home
And back to bed until eleven.
But once a year our weekends
Got a kickstart and a thump,
With that Californian, Saturday morning
Evel Knieval jump.

Stars and Stripes and Lycra-slick,
Gears and engine flexed.
Twenty million tuned in;
(Dickie Davies coming next.)
And while mums and dads and kids
Discuss the minuses and pluses,
Knieval takes our childhood
Over twenty seven buses.

Wheelies

Take my Bowie records and my Star Wars DVDs;
Rip the Berghaus jacket off my back.
Cut my hair, eBay my chair and leave me on my knees
And burn my prized Adidas anorak.

Instant football access in our pockets won't placate us;
Technology ain't what us dads desire.
So eat my sweets, delete my tweets and detonate my status;
The interweb don't set our hearts on fire.

And don't head to the dads' shelves when in search of Christmas
goodies:
A ninja turtle tie won't bring us laughter.
We're not craving Marks and Spencers when we rise on Christmas
morning -
It's those trainers with the wheels on that we're after.

As usual, the kids get all the best stuff Christmas Day,
While we're left with the jumpers and the socks.
Do you see our jealous faces when we're gathered round the tree
And those wheelie shoes are pulled out of the box?

Just imagine me and Geoff and Dave a-skating to the match
Or sliding down the aisles in ASDA shopping.
The pirouettes and spins would surely help our BMI
And work wonders for our secret body-popping.

So let us at those wheelies children! Give us dads a treat!
Rejecting our desires is just a crime.
It was us that gave you skateboards, skateparks, rollerblades and life,
So open up your hearts it's payback time.

Alchemy Dad

Our dad was the DIY wizard.
Got something to fix? Piece of cake.
When locked in the warmth of his garage,
There was nothing that he couldn't make.

He once made a TV antenna
By bending my sister's hair clip.
He even made grandma's false teeth
From some plastic he'd found on a skip.

A piece of old carpet from my room
And some biscuits that lay in the larder
Were woven together like magic
And turned into a blue Ford Granada.

A sock and an old tin of peas
Were transformed into Action Man clothes.
And he made us a scarf and some mittens
From the hairs that grew up his nose.

He spent his days fixing and building;
And nothing for dad was too tough.
Like for Xmas he made us a bike each
From four rusty nails and some fluff.

He never was tempted by shopping;
The family had all heard him shout:
'Why would I spend cash on that rubbish -
When I can make magic for nowt?'

But the best thing he ever created
As I take a look back through the years
Was that day when I grazed both my knees
He made a big smile from my tears.

.

By the Bins

The sultry autumn sunlight streams
Through garden fence in fiery beams,
But lurking like a string of silken sin:
The threaded dreaded wire
Of the spider's dark desire
Waits between the gate and wheelie bin.

And trudging through the early morning,
Sleepy, half-undressed and yawning.
Dad with glass and plastic balanced high.
The debris from the night before
But strung from nature's utmost drawer
The driveway trap for father and for fly.

A flailing, wailing, pirouetting
Dad is caught in nature's netting,
Bound up in tangled yarn of itching.
And dancing like a man possessed,
In falling jeans and untucked vest,
He crawls back to the comfort of the kitchen.

Christmas Crackers

A Shepherd's Tale
Even by the dim light of the candles in the stable,
I could see I'd made a terrible mistake.
A pillowcase of presents by the baby in the cradle
While Joseph and his wife ate Christmas cake.

Expensive looking boxes, shiny paper, fancy ribbon
Shimmered by the manger in the cold.
A jar of oily stuff and a tub of frankincense
Leant against a massive stack of gold.

But Christmas Day's a joke round here, as all the shops are shut
And the weather where I live was turning nasty.
So I legged it to the garage, bought the baby what I could:
A pack of Mini Eggs and a pasty.

In the Foyer

Bunking off maths decorating the tree
In the foyer at Christmas, Amy and me.
Baubles and fairy lights strewn on the floor,
Boxes and plastic bags blocking the door.
Teachers pass by with glances approving;
Time's ticking on, but we're not for moving.
Tied up in tinsel, defying the bell -
If we string this thing out,
We'll miss science as well.

Bagsy That

A change in the temperature, coal-fired air.
Halloween, Bonfire Night, we didn't care.
For what got us through all the gloom and the fog
Were the toys in the back of the Argos catalogue.

Football could wait, forget hide and seek,
Kick the Can, Bulldog - we'll play those next week.
'Cos perched on our wall, under lamp post for ages,
We'd live out our dreams and flick through the pages:

Bagsy that bike. Bagsy that ball.
Collection of Corgi cars - bagsied them all.
Bagsy the Hot Wheels, Subbuteo set,
Lego, Scalextric, badminton net,
Buckaroo, Downfall, Connect 4 and Cluedo,
Risk - bagsied that, Operation and Ludo.

Eyes on that frisbee to throw in the Park,
Millennium Falcon that glows in the dark.
Take all of these treasures from out of my head
To the pillowcase laid at the foot of my bed.

So now in this time of technology magic,
Is it too much to ask for a time-travel gadget?
For if I could go back and relive some sights,
I'd savour the days and I'd bagsy those nights.

Epiphany

A couple of weeks after Christmas,
A 'lock-in' we had at The Crown.
The tree had lost its needles
And the tinsel had fallen down.

Marlene wore a daft hat
And waited for jokes to begin
And Frank had laid on a buffet
To entice the locals in.

Just before eight, three strangers
Arrived and bought three pints of beer.
They gave off an air of intelligence -
And we figured they weren't from round here.

Leanne, she couldn't stop looking
Hypnotised, with her mouth open wide.
They all wore expensive silk dresses
Despite the cold weather outside.

They put down their weird-looking parcels
And huddled round close at the bar
I could tell old George didn't trust them
As he stared at them all from afar.

The tall one sat down in Bob's chair
And I feared he'd end up with a thump.
He smelled a bit like a camel,
And predictably, Bob got the hump.

"We're seeking The Star," he piped up.
"We've travelled to worship the king."
I knew Vince did a good Robbie Williams,
But Elvis was never his thing.

"The Star, love, it's in the next village,"
Chirped Ann with flick of her hair.
"But you'll not get a bus there at this time,
Especially in't dresses you wear."

But before Jim had finished his scratchings,
The quest of the three recommenced.
"What's up with the beer in here?"
With a growl, shouted Frank incensed.

Then we all looked around in wonder
As off to The Star they were sent
And it was as the three camels passed 't window
That it hit me, that's not what they meant.

What Shall We Call Him?

All night in the gloom they had shivered.
The stable, bursting with questions:
"What's this frankincense for
That they've left at the door?
Is myrrh for the feet?
Did they leave a receipt?
Anyone got some suggestions?"

But as for a name for the baby -
Round the manger, a sea of blank faces.
They'd grappled with Gordon
And juggled with Jordan
And couldn't believe it
When Joseph said Steve
It was no way to Barry
And Harry and Gary
But who would have thought this:
That Ken made the shortlist?
I'm sure we'd predict
A David or Benedict
Names sent from heaven
But maybe not Kevin
Or Graham or Des
Or Leonard or Les.
A name for the child
That wasn't too wild.
The parents were both unimpressed.
It was proving a difficult test.

Those present were scraping the barrel
For a name that suited a carol
A name with real power
That wasn't too long
That was nice written down
Sounded good in a song
A name for all time
That couldn't be shortened
Tricky to rhyme
But sounded important.
A name of which he'd be proud.
A name that could pull a huge crowd.

A shepherd that stood 6ft 4
Bumped his head on the frame of the door
Coming in from the night
He misjudged the height
Which was strange as he'd been there before.

"Jesus Christ!" yelled the man with a frown,
As the blood trickled on to his gown.
"That doesn't sound bad,"
Said the son of God's dad. -
"Get a pen Mary, write that one down."

Mystery Chairs

From where do you come, O mystery chairs?
Christmas Day at around two o'clock?
Extendable family, extendable table:
Surprising enough, but how is mum able
To seat the whole sum of her flock?

Oh mystery family history chairs,
How is it you all come about?
Live you beneath coats in a room underground?
Ignored in the loft 'til December comes round?
Does Santa Claus hire you out?

Ah magic pragmatic fantastical chairs
In our midst, when we thought we had none.
Like shepherds to stable,
You come to our table
Then by Boxing Day you are gone.

When Gloves Dry

"I want to go out again mum,
But my gloves and hat are wet.
I put them on the fire guard,
Are they going to be dry enough yet?"

"Go and get some socks," she says,
"And slip them on instead.
That's what we used to do,
And pop your dad's hat on your head."

"I can't do that," I told her,
"I'm not wearing socks on my hands!"
Even at 5 I've got street cred,
But I don't think she understands.

Maybe I'm just too demanding;
Perhaps I just need to try.
But this is what it sounds like
In our house, when gloves dry.

Do They Know it's Not Christmas?

Let's hear it for those die hards; let's celebrate the few
Who, at the death of Christmastime, don't do what others do.
When you and I have kissed the plastic mistletoe goodbye,
Our heroes with their lights still up have bigger sprouts to fry.

They brighten up the bus ride down the road or into town:
These Hark the Herald Angels who refuse to take em down.
While we return those jumpers back to Next and M&S,
They thunder into Springtime on the Santa Claus Express.

But who are they, these renegades so desperate to ignore
The longer days and golden sunshine knocking at the door?
The busy, stressed or lazy or the ones that can't remember?
The ultra-ready family being first for next December?

The looney uni student with his tongue clamped in his cheek?
The tinsel-happy chap who wants to brighten up your week?
The overbearing kids who just can't bear to let it go?
The frail old girl at number twelve that no one got to know.

And do they spend each evening cracking nuts and writing cards?
Reruns of the Queen's Speech and a few games of charades?
Pulling crackers, telling jokes in funny paper hats -
Home time with the family - what's silly about that?

So let's not tut or curl disdainful lips or roll our eyes
As they rock around the tree and count their boxes of mince pies.
Respect their speck of sparkle in this world of dread and fear.
Perhaps to them it's Christmas now, and Christmastime all year.

Last Year's Games

Ignored for months in shadow, under wardrobes, under beds,
Argos sleeping giant almost new.
They picked it up last Boxing Day and looked at it new year,
Then found twelve months of other things to do.

But now that school is over and the big day's coming close
And flailing friends come knocking at the door,
They rise from darkened corners with their sellophane unbroken
And spread their plastic pieces on my floor.

See them hover round the virgin, multicoloured board
Like kids around the new girl in the yard.
They squabble over rule-books, statuettes and who goes first,
A spinner and a million bits of card.

But soon the dice are rolling and the party's going strong,
Oblivious to what they soon will get.
I journey from the kitchen bearing gifts of custard creams
For children that I've never even met.

And last years' chosen games are resurrected for the day,
As they kneel around the figures as in prayer.
But with their lids replaced they know they're destined for the loft
To be born again at next year's Christmas Fair.

Affray in a Manger

Every mum and dad I know have got a birthing story:
A thirty-hour labour with an emphasis on gory;
A Cressida or Clementine arriving on a boat,
A baby in the fast lane, on the taxi driver's coat.

A birth at 30,000 feet above the English Channel;
Delivery in the bathroom when you've only got a flannel.
A trauma in the traffic after climbing in the car,
A cherub in the salon, after twinges in the Spar.

But gather all ye faithful, hear the tale I bring to table,
That started on a donkey and ended in a stable.
A starry night in Bethlehem - O busy little town;
Some shepherds wearing dirty tea-towels seated all around.

The B&Bs were full that night so we were in a state;
Some Christian convention got the rooms at discount rate.
But a scruffy little number, not much bigger than a shack
Had a drafty little shed thing past the toilets out the back.

So we tied the knackered donkey to a broken wheelie bin,
Took a deep breath, grabbed our bags and shyly shuffled in.
The room, it wasn't comfy, but we knew we had to stay.
And I searched it for a kettle or some biscuits on a tray.

Or a telly or a WiFi linked to hotel internet
Or shower gel or those cute little shampoos that you get.
No chocolates on a pillow in this tiny little shed,
And even our new baby had a straw box for a bed.

So when I heard our lass' shortened breaths intensify
And the baby made his entrance as the star hung in the sky,
We wrapped the little bundle in a cardigan I wore,
As those nosey tea-towelled shepherds poked their heads in through
the door.

Before too long a woman from the pub dragged in a tree
And a box of decorations and a Christmas hits CD.
And before we knew it, all the cows and every little lamb
Were bopping round to Shakin' Stevens, Slade and Cliff and Wham.

Some blokes in gowns and crowns arrived to add to all the fun;
And brought three fancy presents when some nappies would have
done.
Two bowed down and one was acting like a bodyguard,
And we all began to look like we were on a Christmas card.

The night became chaotic then and we began to flip;
With angels dancing on the roof it's hard to get some kip.
So I stormed across the courtyard to the pub and grabbed the boss
And let him know the world's first virgin mum was at a loss.

I was furious and told him that the stable thing was dire,
Not suitable at all to introduce the new Messiah.
But he shouted, "Don't blame me sunshine, for all this hurlyburly.
"It's Christmas Eve for Christ's sake mate, you should have booked in
early."

Brass

The brass band in the entrance up at Tesco's pulls a crowd
With Jingle Bells and Winter Wonderland.
Shiny trumpets, Santa hats, a woman with a bucket.
And tinsel blu-tacked on each music stand.

We block the door and let them lead us back to yuletides past;
They remind us what this season is about.
But Christmas cheer is stopped when we remember why we're there,
As we slip into the shop and give 'em nowt.

Boxed

So there they go, the decorations.
Bleak midwinter's exclamations.
Cards unpegged and lights untangled,
Tinsel, baubles now undangled.
Bells unjingled, kids untingled,
Buffet tables disem-pringled.
Gifts are hoarded, games cardboarded,
Stacks of plastic unafforded,
Call the Midwife prerecorded.
eBay raided, phone upgraded,
Slade and Bandaid over-playeded.
Multicoloured wrap recycled,
Radio stations un-GeorgeMichaeled,
Tesco's foyer band disbanded,
Father Christmas re-Laplanded.
TV pull-outs disregarded.
All December credit-carded -
Calculations microsofted.
Another Christmas boxed and lofted.

School Days

A Shiver in the Park

We head across the field when mum allows us.
But the big kids with their love bites, hair and fags and baggy trousers
Are crowding round our climbing frame and hanging on our pole,
And our woolly hats and lollies ain't what they call rock and roll.
So we try to find a way onto the see-saws and the slides,
But they don't give a damn about the fun that they provide.
They just sit around and smoke and sneer and snog and other things:
They're the rulers of the roundabout, the sultans of the swings.

Play and Record

It may be a little bit naughty
To record the nation's top forty,
But this love affair is tangled in our hearts.
We couldn't do without it,
But the hardest thing about it
Is stopping the tape before the speaking st..

Bestest Dinner Lady

Diva of the dinner time,
She's something else is Barbara.
Resplendent in those earrings
Like an antique candelabra.
She brightens up your Monday
Like a day trip up to Scarborough
She's our favourite dinner lady
Is Barbara.

When other teachers let you down
And fail to understand;
When the day is turning out
Not exactly as you planned
Go and have a chat with Barbara,
Mug of coffee in her hand.
She'll pick you up and make you smile
Will Barbara.

Barbara's got the gossip
And Barbara knows the score.
And Barbara's got that look
That says that she's seen it all before.
And she smuggles us free cake
So she's the one that we adore
She's the bestest dinner lady
Is Barbara.

Cut the Mustard

There wasn't much to beat the volleyed, last gasp winning goal,
Or top mark in the weekly spelling test.
Or Friday in assembly when you picked up those awards
That proved to kids at school you were best.

Not much topped the moment when she read your story out
And the clapping echoed through the class for hours.
And don't forget the day when that old lady came to visit
And Miss decided you could give her flowers.

But all of this just paled next to that moment in the hall,
When none of the above could cut the mustard.
'Cos the icing on the cake was when the big kids on your table
Granted you the skin from off the custard.

Pink Custard

How did you get there, oh custard of pink?
Transported by little green men?
Why did the government deal in this stuff?
Was there no Health and Safety back then?

Were you mixed in the jars on the easels in class?
Were you bound in the caretaker's shed?
Oh wallpaper paste; oh nuclear waste -
Did the cat throw you up on its bed?

Do you ooze from the bark of a prickly tree?
Do you spawn in the mouth of the Nile?
Are you poisonous maybe? Or alien gravy?
Or glue from the arts and craft pile?

We remember you shaking poured over the cake
Of us innocent, underweight creatures.
If your chemical make-up of gloop was nutritious,
Then why were you shunned by the teachers?

Sharp

Clamped on Miss' desk, like a robot from the future,
The handled, hungry sharp'ner slyly lingers.
It's half-gaped silver mouth appears to whisper to our class
As we try to keep our thoughts on counting fingers.

And Miss says we can try it for a treat this rainy morning,
Just before she turfs us all outdoors.
So me and Billy leg it past our classmates to the front
And gaze into its slightly open jaws.

Then we wait for Miss to walk away to help another
And we sharpen minds to do the thing we must:
While jealous friends stare open-mouthed and Miss is on her knees,
We shave those coloured pencils into dust.

Dark Arts

Only some are chosen
And few accept the mission
Of cradling and passing on
The art of long division.

They borrow here and pay back there,
These children of Set 1,
While we run out of fingers
To meekly count upon.

Up and down the kingdom,
From town to ocean wide,
We wallow in defeat
As they conquer and divide.

Unexpected

Like lambs to the slaughter, we couldn't believe it
The news that the smart ones suspected:
That Sponge and Aunt Spiker, and Boggis and Bean
And that Sunday night girl were connected.

Curtains drawn, dressing gown, 9.45
That dancer gyrating on red.
And just when we thought we were safe on the sofa,
Mum would chime: "Right, up to bed."

He's ours though, not theirs! We read him at school!
James and that magical peach.
How could it be then our man could have written
These things that were now out of reach?

Like spying your dad with a stocking of presents,
Or tooth under pillow rejected.
Let's not understate the blow to the head
From this come-of-age tale unexpected.

Chess Club

Early lunch pass gets them through.
(While we hang hungry in the queue.)
Then see them manoeuvre to English 2
To Chess Club.

In Chess Club there's some tables set.
Mystic figures. Statuettes.
The thinking prefect's cigarette
Is Chess Club.

Horses, castles, queens and kings,
Prawns and priests and other things.
Need a degree in Lord of the Rings
For Chess Club.

What happens there, we'd love to know.
We'd have that intellectual glow
If we were smart enough to go
To Chess Club.

Nitty Nora the Bug Explorer

Nitty Nora, Nitty Nora -
That's the name that we've got for her.
Could be Linda; could be Laura.
Maybe Donna, Dawn or Dora.
Surely she knows what we call her -
She's the doctor with an aura.
Scratch your head, bow down before her -
Nitty Nora, bug explorer.

Down the hallway, past reception
Where we had that last injection,
Where the sick kids with infection
Go for 'back to maths' rejection -
That's where Nitty Nora lingers;
Eagle eyes and probing fingers
Picking over blondes and gingers.
Teacher with her list will bring us.
If she finds 'owt, school will ring us.

Nora of the nitty gritty.
Nora of this little ditty
Sent by NHS committee,
Combing through the inner city.
Nitty Nora, Nitty Nora.
Raise that playtime milk up for her.
Midgey, moggy, maggot curer:
Nitty Nora, bug explorer.

Ghost Writer

Our teacher in maths was a ghost
And as we filed in lesson two,
We discovered the big kids weren't lying
And the tale that they told us was true.

An icy cold chill filled the classroom
As a weird sound came from the hall.
And we watched with our chins on the tables
As she floated straight in through the wall.

She stood like a god by the whiteboard
And said, "Fill in the graph on page ten.
Does everyone get what we're doing?
Or shall I go through it again?"

Triple Games

When it came to triple games, Mr Thingy gave us choice -
A teacher from the future who believed we had a voice.
Anyone for badminton? Our hands shot up as one.
So we crowded in the gym and turned the radiators on.

Stand and have a natter on the baseline with your mate.
An hour for you to drift away; no need to concentrate.
Not one of us could hit the thing and no-one knew the score -
We got our fitness picking up that white thing from the floor.

So gird your broken spirit and grip that broken racquet;
Ignore your teacher's good advice, just throw it up and smack it.
You'll never find you're lost for breath; you'll never strain your heart:
It's the furthest thing from PE, after chess and double art.

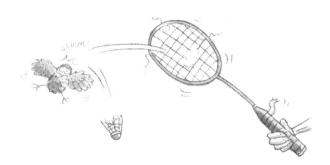

Sick Kid

From double science on the first floor,
Sick boy with his pass in hand,
Eyes turned downwards, no expression
Staggers into no man's land.
Puts on his Thursday pallid face
And in the sick room takes his place.

Five already sit in silence.
Stomachs whine and noses blow.
All of them grip paper towels -
A green-faced, heavy-breathed tableau.
How long before the nurse detects
That all of them have PE next.

Bonjewer Mushewer

Jean-Paul et Marie-France, Professeur Lafayette -
It's time that you et moi sat down and had a tete a tete.
For dans l'ecole, two times a week, we lined up by the door
And came out one hour later, knowing what we knew before.

Our crime against our garlic cousins happened in room huit.
With heads bowed low, we allezed in and shyly took our seats.
She tried her best to make us understand a different route,
But we just dreamt of frites and meat and pomme de terre en croute.

We knew you from the Trifle Tower, World Cup, 'Allo 'Allo,
The onions and the fancy bread, but never planned to go.
We gazed out the fenetre, or we cowered at the back
As our teacher rolled les yeux and took us up a cul de sac.

Ecoutez et repetez you crooned from that recorder
And Frenchly mocked our lacking north of England speech disorder.
That new and deep romantic sexy nasal intonation
You tried to switch us on to couldn't hold our concentration.

That tattered Francais text book where you slyly lay in wait;
Those posters sur la wall avec le verbs to conjugate.
Papa est dans le jardin et Claudette est sur la bus.
Jean-Paul is laughing with his friends and making fun of us.

Perhaps the fear of failure threw our learning to the wall
For rolling 'r's and that, we never had the Charles de Gaulle.
Our teacher, Mrs Something, pulled her hair, and she kept digging,
But had her work cut out for her, teaching French in Wigan.

With gritted teeth, she sang to us and gave us games to play,
And tried to shape our petit minds the European way.
But then that day she found her continental dreams extinguished:
"I can't teach you lot French," she said, "You can't speak bloody
                                                        English."

University Challenged

There's always the one with a bow-tie and glasses
From top of the physics and chemistry classes.
Then there's the girl with a masters in genes,
A doctorate in Latin, whatever that means.
A bloke in a waistcoat that could be Chinese,
A kid with some milk teeth and four PHDs.
A lad with a beard and his hand on the button:
Expert in Tolstoy and Vladimir Putin(!)

A woman from York has me under her spell;
A Giles or a Miles doing Law at Brunel.
The little one stuck on the end saying nowt;
A kid with his cardigan on inside out.
The lad who reads Milton and Dante and Spenser.
The red-headed girl with a pass-out from MENSA.
I try to keep up with my Art CSE
But even the mascot is smarter than me.
So on Mondays I sit there from starter to gong,
And wait for a question on eighties' love songs.

Printed in Great Britain
by Amazon

59344576R00054